The
Problem
Solvers

The Problem Solvers

by Nathan Aaseng

Lerner Publications Company
Minneapolis

Page one: John Deere manufactured two steel plows in 1838. By 1843, he was producing 400 plows a year.

Page two: Edwin Land's associate, George Wheelwright, demonstrates two Polaroid filters in 1939.

Library of Congress Cataloging-in-Publication Data

Aaseng, Nathan
    The problem solvers / by Nathan Aaseng.
        p.   cm.
    Includes index.
    Summary: Discusses how individuals with insight and curiosity
were able to form successful companies by finding creative solutions
to problems.
    ISBN 0-8225-0675-0
    1. Business—Biography—Juvenile literature. 2. Problem
solving—Juvenile literature. [1. Businessmen. 2. Problem
solving.] I. Title.
HC29.A24   1989
338′.04′0922—dc19
[B]
[920]   88-695
                                                  CIP
                                                   AC

Manufactured in the United States of America

1 2 3 4 5 6 7 8 9 10 99 98 97 96 95 94 93 92 91 90 89

To Brian

Contents

John H. Breck tried to find a way to stop his balding and eventually launched a successful line of Breck hair products.

Introduction

A YOUNG MAN IN WILLIMANSETT, Massachusetts, didn't like what he saw in the mirror. He was losing hair so fast he was likely to be bald by the time he was 30.

Seeking medical advice, the man was told that little was known about hair and scalp problems. When it came to hair treatment, consumers were at the mercy of home remedies.

During the time when the man began shedding hair, an entirely different problem was bothering cotton producers in the southern United States. One of the by-products of cotton production, the oil from the seeds, was as good as a fine vegetable oil except for two flaws: it smelled horrible and tasted even worse! Cottonseed oil was occasionally fed to cattle, but it was virtually a waste product.

A young chemist wondered if he could remove the component in the oil that was creating the unpleasantness.

You don't even need to know the entire stories of these two men to know if they were successful in solving the problems that confronted them. All you need to know are their names: the balding man was John Breck; the chemist was David Wesson. The problems they tackled led to two successful, well-known business enterprises—Breck hair products and Wesson Oil.

The stories in this book will show that today's problems can become tomorrow's corporations. A person with a creative, inventive mind might discover a new product where someone else just sees an annoyance.

Problems offer for free something that many businesspersons work hard and spend a lot of money to create—a demand or "market." The more frustrating and widespread the problem, the greater the demand for a product that can end the frustration. A person who sees the problem as an opportunity and develops an affordable solution to it will have a ready-made market of consumers eager to buy the product.

The stories of Breck and Wesson illustrate two very different problems and solutions. Breck's hair loss was a personal problem that he wanted to solve for his own peace of mind. He did research in public libraries and experimented in his own home.

Breck was not able to accomplish his original

David Wesson

objective, to cure his own baldness. But he did learn enough about hair care to treat hair and scalp problems. Eventually he formulated products designed to promote hair care and, more than 20 years after he became concerned about his thinning hair, John H. Breck Inc. was on its way to becoming a nationally known business.

David Wesson, on the other hand, was a professional. A graduate of the Massachusetts Institute of Technology, he had done a lot of research in chemistry. In 1900, only a year after establishing a laboratory to work on the cottonseed oil problem, Wesson found his answer, a process that gave the oil a neutral smell and taste. His product, Wesson Oil, became the first vegetable oil used for cooking and has been popular ever since.

Some of the corporations and products in this book, such as the Kitchen-Aid dishwasher, were built by amateurs like Breck. Some, like the Polaroid camera and the Evinrude motor, were developed by people as highly trained as Wesson. Others, such as John Deere and Prudential Insurance, were started out of efforts to help neighbors solve their problems. Still others, such as AstroTurf, were attempts to solve business problems.

What started for some people as problems to be solved ended up as products and companies. This book tells the stories of these creative businesspeople and their products.

A Sticky Problem for Farmers

John Deere

TIRED OF WRESTLING WITH THE ROCKY, stump-cluttered soil of New England, farmers in the early 19th century often followed rumors of better land to the midwestern United States. There, in states such as Illinois and Iowa, they found just what they were looking for: prairies full of rich, black dirt that promised to pump life into seeds as fast as they were planted.

Unfortunately, many settlers soon felt like thirsty sailors in the middle of the ocean—water everywhere but not a drop to drink. Rich soil surrounded them, but their equipment could not plow it. That was the problem a blacksmith named John Deere faced when he arrived in Grand Detour, Illinois, in 1836.

Deere was born in Rutland, Vermont, in 1804. After a public school education, he was apprenticed to a blacksmith in Middlebury, Vermont, at the age of 17. He learned his lessons well. The high-quality ironwork he produced for a local sawmill put his services in demand throughout the Vermont countryside. At the age of 21, he completed his training and struck out on his own. Especially skilled at fashioning highly polished shovels and pitchforks, the traveling blacksmith attracted enough business from merchants and farmers to support his mother and his own growing family. Even though his shop burned to the ground twice, Deere was able to run a successful business for a dozen years.

In the mid-1830s, however, many farmers grew tired of struggling with the rocky Vermont soil. Many of Deere's customers headed west in search of better job prospects. Leaving his wife and four children behind temporarily, Deere packed up to join a group of former neighbors who had settled in Grand Detour, Illinois.

His Illinois neighbors had been desperate for a blacksmith ever since they had settled in Grand Detour. No sooner did Deere set foot in town than he found a line of farmers eager to offer him business. Two days after his arrival in Grand Detour, he was hard at work fixing broken equipment.

While working at his shop, Deere frequently heard complaints from farmers about the soil. Their early excitement about the richness of the soil and the ease with which a plow could break the sod had turned to frustration. The soil was too rich. Instead of

In the 19th century, a young person often became an **apprentice** to a skilled worker to learn a skill or trade like blacksmithing. The apprentice worked for little money but gained experience. Today, most people go to a college, university, or vocational school to learn a skill.

falling away from the plow like sandy New England soil, it stuck. Farmers had to stop every few seconds to scrape the clumped dirt off their iron plowshares with large wooden paddles. They might as well have been plowing through a rocky field for all the progress they were making. Some farmers were so discouraged by the sticky soil that they left in search of new land; others were ready to join them.

Deere decided to look into the problem. From his previous work on plows, he knew that dirt was less likely to stick to highly polished metal. That thought was in the back of his mind when he visited a sawmill in 1837 and noticed a broken circular saw made of steel, a polished metal that was too expensive to be widely used for implements. Steel had never been used to make a plowshare.

Deere took the broken saw blade home with him and began working on a better plow. He knew that polished steel was not the whole answer; the shape of the plow's bottom was also important.

The plow Deere wanted to make would have to cut deeply into the soil at a sharp angle so that dirt would fall off, yet it could not put too much burden on the horses pulling it. After some experiments, Deere found the curved shape he needed and pounded the steel saw blade into that shape. He then built a plow, complete with oak handles, and brought it to the farm of his neighbor, Lewis Crandall.

While an anxious crowd of Grand Detour farmers watched, Crandall tried the new plow. He pronounced

John Deere

John Deere insisted on making high-quality plows: "I will not put my name on a product that does not have in it the best that is in me," he said.

it a success. Not only did dirt fall away cleanly from the blade, but the plow also turned the soil more quickly than the old cast-iron plows.

Other farmers wanted one of Deere's "self-scouring" plows. The blacksmith could not meet the instant demand, however. For one thing, polished steel was hard to find. Deere could not count on a steady supply of broken saw blades to use as raw material. Steel was only available from England, and it was expensive to import. There was no such thing as mass production in the blacksmithing business; plows were made one at a time according to each customer's

A basic rule of business involves supply and demand. The number of products that are offered for sale at different prices at a certain time is called **supply**. **Demand** is the number of products that people are willing to buy at different prices at a certain time. Since John Deere could not make very many plows at a time, demand was greater than supply.

The word **production** refers to all activities involved in converting natural resources, such as iron or trees, into finished goods, or products, such as plows or wood or paper. (Natural resources occur in nature—they are not made by humans.) **Mass production** is the production of goods in large quantities. Mass-produced items are each made alike. The jobs necessary to make the product are broken into small parts, and machines may do most of the work of people. **Manufacturing** refers to the making of articles by hand or with machines. John Deere manufactured his plows, but he did not mass-produce them.

needs. Deere and his new partner in the business, Leonard Andrus, manufactured only 2 "self-scouring" plows in 1838 and 10 the following year.

Production gradually increased, however, as Deere imported greater quantities of expensive English steel. Forty handmade plows left his shop in 1840 and, after expanding his workshop to include a foundry in 1843, Deere's production rose to 400 plows a year.

Until then, Deere still considered himself a blacksmith—his plow was just one part of his craft. But after seeing that he could easily sell as many plows as he could make, even using costly English steel, the blacksmith decided to devote his time to manufacturing plows. In 1846 he found a Pittsburgh steel firm that could supply him with all the steel he needed for a lower price than what the English steel cost. The following year, he moved his business to Moline, Illinois, where the Mississippi River provided water power and transportation.

During the early years, Deere's sales strategy consisted of loading a wagon with plows and visiting farms until all his merchandise was sold. He rarely had to travel far. Producing plows before they were ordered was an innovative approach to sales. By 1857 the company, which he had reorganized with new partners under the name John Deere & Company, was making and selling 10,000 plows a year—nearly seven times as many as he had sold just seven years earlier.

A relentless perfectionist, Deere kept tinkering with his plows, trying to make them better. He came out with 10 new versions of his plow in a single year. While this slowed down his production ability, it ensured Deere a solid reputation among his customers. Deere plows became world famous in the 1870s when they outshone the competition in a demonstration in France. That same decade, the company built its first riding plow and designed the leaping deer as its trademark.

John Deere died in 1886, but his company has gone on to become one of the most recognized names in farm equipment. Following the furrow laid by the Vermont blacksmith who made it possible for his neighbors to continue farming, Deere & Company now produces more than 600 labor-saving products.

An important concern for businesses is to develop the best possible product and continue to improve the product. If another company could develop and sell a better product for the same price, customers would go to that company. John Deere understood the need to make the best possible product. "If we don't improve our product, somebody else will, and we will lose our trade," he said.

Protection
for the Poor

Prudential

John Dryden

IF ALL THE PROBLEMS IN THE BUSI-ness world could be solved by the invention of new machinery, then engineers and scientists would be running every corporation in the country. But many problems have nothing to do with tools, gadgets, or laboratory testing. Sometimes a creative new law, economic plan, or attitude can change life for the better as dramatically as any labor-saving device.

The insurance plan developed by John Dryden more than 100 years ago is one example of an innovation that didn't involve machines. Before Dryden went into business, life insurance was a privilege of the rich. Ordinary working-class people simply could not afford it. The people who would be plunged hopelessly into debt by the death of the family breadwinner could not protect themselves with insurance. At the same time, the rich could receive insurance protection for costs they could easily afford.

The founder of The Prudential Insurance Company of America experienced the unfair system firsthand when he was young. John Dryden was born in Temple Mills, Maine, in 1839. John's father worked as a mechanic and, although he received enough wages to purchase his own home, he did not earn enough to build any kind of savings account. When he died in 1849, his family had no money set aside to pay their bills.

As a result, John's childhood ended abruptly when he was 10. It was replaced by a dreary fight for survival. He got up early every morning to work as a delivery boy for a bakery, attended school all day, then reported for a second job as a mechanic's assistant. This brutal schedule nearly ruined his health, but he endured it long enough to graduate from high school.

After graduation Dryden took a full-time job as a mechanic. Unlike most other struggling wage earners of the time, he refused to give up his hope for a college education. Dryden set aside as much savings as he could and finally, in 1861, he had accumulated enough money to attend Yale University.

For one of his research projects at school, he charted the history of the Prudential Assurance Company. This London-based company had introduced industrial insurance in 1854 and had met with

Insurance is a way to cover the cost of unexpected losses —such as deaths, accidents, or fires—by dividing the cost of the loss among many individuals. An insured person doesn't have to pay the whole cost of the loss himself or herself—the insurance company pays it. Insurance works because a large group of people (the insured) pay a **premium** (a regular payment of money) to the insurance company. This provides the company with a large amount of money available to cover the losses. For example, say that Jane pays $500 a year for automobile insurance. She has an accident and the repairs cost $3,000. Her $500 is not enough to cover the costs, but because thousands of people pay $500 a year for insurance, the company has enough to pay for the repairs.

Workers put in long hours sewing garments at a clothing factory. Concerned about the plight of the factory worker, John Dryden worked to develop an insurance plan that working-class people could afford.

A person's **savings** is the money he or she has set aside for future use. Many people place their savings in a **savings account** at a bank.

surprising success. Industrial insurance was low-cost insurance for workers. It usually paid just enough to bury someone. Because of his own background, Dryden was intrigued by the idea of insurance for the common worker, and he filed away information on the subject.

By his senior year at Yale, Dryden had proved himself one of the school's best students and had made plans for a career in law. But Dryden was forced to drop out of school just as his dreams were about to come true. Less than a year away from college graduation, his health broke down under the strain of long years of overwork. He and his new wife moved to Ohio to stay with a sister while he recovered.

When he was ready to resume work, Dryden took a job with an insurance company. He began by selling the standard life insurance then in existence, but the insurance company he worked for failed, and he moved back east in 1866. While selling insurance in Brooklyn, New York, he began working on making insurance available to low-paid workers.

It took him several years to find a partner to support his plan financially. When he finally did, the state of New York refused to grant his insurance company a charter (a license to sell insurance). Undaunted, Dryden moved to Newark, New Jersey, and tried again.

Most businesspersons scoffed at Dryden's ideas. Workers could not afford to pay more than a few pennies per week for insurance. Analysts did not see how any company could survive on such low income. At last Dryden did convince two influential people— the landlord of the office space he was renting and a physician concerned with social issues—that his plan had merit. Even with their backing, it wasn't until 1875 that the Prudential Friendly Society, named after the British company, finally opened for business.

Dryden faced enormous problems. He spent long hours devising life expectancy charts and computing insurance fees based on those figures. Fraudulent insurance schemes were common, and Dryden had to persuade a wary public that his business was

An insurance company does not have to pay for too many losses all at once. This can be explained by the **law of large numbers**, or the law of averages. According to this mathematical rule, out of a very large number of similar risks (such as the risk of having an automobile accident), only a certain number of losses will actually occur. In other words, although each of the many people who pay for automobile insurance *could* have an accident, only a certain number of them *will* have one. That number can be predicted. By calculating the number of losses that will likely occur to the group of insured people during a given amount of time, an insurance company knows how much money (called a rate) each insured person must pay.

If you are in **debt**, it means that you owe someone something. Debt is an obligation to pay something. A company or individual goes into **bankruptcy** when they cannot pay their debts.

A **claim** is the evidence of loss (death, accident, etc.) the insured gives to the company when he or she wants the company to pay for the loss.

A company is said to make a **profit** when the money it earns from sales amounts to more than the cost of producing the goods or service. Profit can also be seen as the reward that the business-person receives for taking the risk of investing time and money in an enterprise. In the United States, the possibility of earning a profit is an important motive for entering business.

honest. He spoke to workers at factories during lunch breaks and met with them after working hours, and he hunted carefully for good insurance agents to sell his product.

During its first year, Dryden's company sold fewer than 300 policies. Because the company promised to pay all claims promptly and without dispute, it often faced serious financial problems. In 1876 the company teetered on the brink of bankruptcy. When a policyholder named Mrs. Glover became critically ill, Prudential seemed doomed to fail. If she were to die, the $500 the company would have to pay to her survivors would drive Dryden out of business.

Fortunately for Mrs. Glover, the company's precarious financial position meant that its founders took a personal interest in her health. Dr. Leslie Ward, a member of the board of directors, rushed to Mrs. Glover's house. He nursed her back to health, and the company was saved, along with Mrs. Glover.

Dryden then traveled to England to get advice from the original Prudential company about how to make the system work. With this new information, he reorganized his company, now called The Prudential Insurance Company, and it finally began to show profits. By 1879 it sold nearly 45,000 policies. Seven years later, more than two million people owned a "piece of the rock"—the Rock of Gibraltar, which the company uses as its symbol of strength.

Of more lasting importance than Prudential's sales figures was the effect that Prudential had on the availability of insurance for low-income workers. In 1875 less than two percent of the United States' population owned life insurance. The death of a family breadwinner usually meant extreme poverty for the family and a pauper's grave for the deceased. By 1911 Prudential alone was insuring more than 10 million individuals. Several other companies followed Prudential into the low-cost insurance market. John Dryden saved many United States families from having to endure the harsh conditions that had made his own childhood so difficult.

1896

1920s

1950s

Prudential's symbol, the Rock of Gibraltar, changed in appearance over the years.

1984

Good Help Was Too Hard to Find

Kitchen-Aid Dishwasher

ON THE AVERAGE, EACH PERSON IN the United States uses dishes about 2.5 million times in his or her lifetime. Who washes all those dishes? One hundred years ago, the answers might have been you, your children, or a servant.

Now there is an easier option, far less expensive than a servant. You can pack all of the dishes into a dishwasher, press a button, and let the machine do the work.

The person who built the first practical automatic dishwasher was not an inventor, a professional engineer, a hard-working mechanic, or even someone fed up with doing dishes and determined to end that drudgery.

The unlikely inventor of the automatic dishwasher was a wealthy woman named Josephine Garis

Although Josephine Garis Cochrane never had to wash dishes herself, she invented the first automatic dishwasher.

Cochrane. She was not at all concerned with saving labor; she simply wanted to save her good dishes from careless servants.

Josephine Garis Cochrane was so pampered that she scarcely had to wash or fix or clean anything. The daughter of a well-to-do civil engineer in Chicago, she grew up in a luxurious home, surrounded by servants who took care of the household tasks.

Although marriage carried Cochrane away from the glamour of the big city to the small town of Shelbyville in central Illinois, she remained pampered. Her husband was an influential figure in Illinois politics during the 1880s, and an invitation to the Cochranes' home was highly prized by many people. Josephine's upbringing served her well in providing the kind of elegant entertainment that was expected in such company. She was used to directing the energies of a houseful of servants.

During formal gatherings, the Cochranes served dinner on Josephine's expensive, imported china. Unfortunately, after several of these dinners, her set of china had suffered alarming casualties at the hands of her servants. Most of the damage occurred during the dishwashing. Each time Mrs. Cochrane discovered another chip or crack in a piece of china, she ordered the servants to be more careful with her dishes. She could not understand why no one had invented some kind of automatic dishwasher that would protect her valuable dishes from careless handling.

No matter what she said, though, china kept getting ruined. Finally she decided that, if no one else would save her dishes for her, she would save them herself. She would invent an automatic dishwasher.

Actually, a few such contraptions had been built before this time. As early as 1850, a New York man was granted a patent for a wooden machine that splashed water on dishes. His crude invention, however, was never taken seriously.

Although she had never worked with machinery, Josephine set up shop in the family woodshed. Asking for advice when she needed it, she eventually came up with the basic design which dishwashers follow to this day. She twisted wire in the shape of a rack and attached it to a wire wheel. Then she placed the

In the 20th century, many appliances have been developed which save labor, or work, in the home. Besides dishwashers, some labor-saving appliances are washing machines, dryers, can openers, blenders, and food processors.

rack in a boxlike compartment and mounted it on top of a copper wash boiler (a tank full of hot water). A handcrank caused the rack—which was loaded with dishes—to spin around. At the same time, hot, soapy water pumped out of the boiler and showered over the dishes.

It wasn't an attractive appliance and, because the crank had to be turned by hand, it did not save much labor. But it really could clean dishes. Josephine named it the "Garis-Cochrane" and showed it off to her friends. Since many of them were influential people, word quickly spread about what she had accomplished. When restaurants and hotels began to contact her about the "Garis-Cochrane," Josephine decided to go into business. She received a patent in December of 1886 and set up a company to produce dishwashers.

Cochrane directed the company, eventually known as the Crescent Washing Machine Company, until her death in 1913. Although she built her first dishwasher for her own home use, she concentrated her marketing efforts on hotels, restaurants, and institutions. Her company did produce the first automatic dishwasher designed for home use. The design was bought in 1926 by the Hobart Manufacturing Company, a food equipment manufacturer, now a part of P.M.I. Food Equipment Group. But the dishwasher required far more hot water than most homes could produce. Interest among consumers for an automatic dishwasher was lukewarm, at best.

Marketing is the process of developing a product, determining how much it should cost, deciding how it should be sold, and making sure that people who want to buy the product can get it. One slogan describes marketing as "finding a need and filling it."

This early model dishwasher bears little resemblance to its modern counterpart.

It was not until 1949 that Hobart produced a successful line of home dishwashers. The company's market research showed that guilt was the main reason people shied away from dishwashers. Women, especially, felt that it was a bad reflection on them if they spent money on something they could do themselves.

Hobart finally solved the problem by advertising that the Kitchen-Aid brand dishwasher used water which was hotter than humans could stand and which was therefore more effective at killing germs. The new ads eased people's guilt and more people bought automatic dishwashers. Today automatic dishwashers are used in about half the home kitchens in the United States, and the Kitchen-Aid brand, originated by Josephine Cochrane, remains one of the industry leaders. It never would have happened if Josephine's servants had not broken her good china.

An important part of marketing is listening to what customers say about a product. By finding out why consumers did not use dishwashers, the Hobart Manufacturing Company was able to change its advertising to answer consumers' concerns. Peter Drucker, author of several popular books about business, writes, "Marketing is the whole business seen from the view point of its final result, that is, from the customer's point of view."

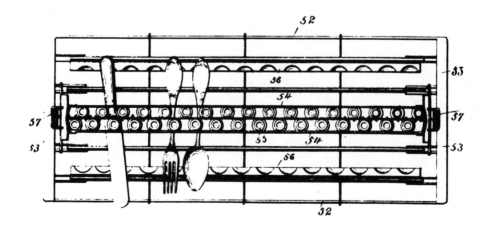

Battle of the Currents

Westinghouse

W E TAKE IT FOR GRANTED THAT, IF
we need energy to operate our appliances or lights,
we can safely plug an electrical cord into an outlet
or flip on a light switch.

At one time, however, such an act was too ter-
rifying for the president of the United States to
attempt. Benjamin Harrison occupied the White
House when electric lights were first installed in
the building in 1889. Neither he nor his wife,
Caroline, dared touch the switches for fear of electrocution. After a servant turned on the hall lights
in the evening, the lights would stay on until some
brave soul turned them off in the morning. The
president and his wife prepared for bed in the dark,
rather than risk turning on a light in their room.

The man most responsible for bringing electricity

Thomas A. Edison

George Westinghouse

safely into the home was an energetic inventor named George Westinghouse. In his efforts to make electricity a household convenience, Westinghouse faced three obstacles. First, he had to overcome the dangers involved in transmitting high-voltage electricity. Second, he had to conquer people's fears of using electricity. Third, he had to beat competitors who were also trying to find solutions to the problem. Among those competitors was a rival so formidable that few inventors would challenge him: Thomas A. Edison.

While Edison is considered one of the greatest inventors of all time, Westinghouse was also a prolific inventor. Westinghouse became so adept at solving problems that he collected more than 350 patents during his career.

Westinghouse was born in Central Bridge, New

George Westinghouse received almost 400 U.S. patents in his life. If you invent a machine or a device, you may apply for a patent. A **patent** is the exclusive right to own, use, and dispose of an invention. The U.S. Patent Office issues more than 1,200 patents each week. Patents for inventions are granted to the owner for 17 years; then the patent expires.

G. WESTINGHOUSE, Jr.
ROTARY STEAM ENGINE.

No. 50,759.　　Patented Oct. 31, 1865.

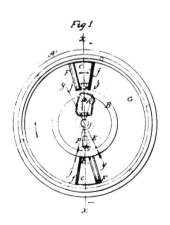

York, in 1846. As a child, he was far more of a problem than a problem solver. George would lie, scheme, hide, and throw frightful tantrums to be allowed to hang around his father's farm implement factory.

When George was 10, his father moved the plant to Schenectady, New York. In Schenectady the boy conspired with one of the factory employees to set up his own workshop in an unused attic. By watching employees working on their equipment and by taking apart machines and putting them back together, George became a master mechanic.

The relentless determination that had made George such a nuisance to his family paid off when the boy began to attack engineering problems. By the age of 19, he had built an automatic pipe-cutting machine and secured his first patent, for a rotary steam engine. He later designed a meter to measure the amount of water used by utilities customers.

Westinghouse frequently traveled by train on business assignments for his father. In those days, when a train built up speed there was no quick way of stopping it. Even a large crew of brakemen applying heavy brake shoes against the wheels to slow them could not stop a speeding train in less than a mile. As a result, head-on collisions sometimes occurred.

After seeing a terrible crash, Westinghouse decided there must be a better way of stopping trains. At the age of 22, he perfected a compressed-air brake with which one person could stop a train quickly. He eagerly offered his invention to railroad companies. In 1868 a small railroad company agreed to give his invention a trial run on a passenger train traveling from Pittsburgh, Pennsylvania, to Steubenville, Ohio.

A twist of fate put Westinghouse's invention to the ultimate test on its very first trip. Coming out of a tunnel in Pittsburgh, the unscheduled train surprised a drayman (a man on a horse pulling a cart) attempting to cross the track. When his horse bolted, the man was thrown in front of the onrushing train. The engineer quickly turned the air valve, and the train ground to a halt within a few feet of the fallen man. Had the train been equipped with a traditional braking system, the man would have been dead.

Backed by this powerful evidence, Westinghouse obtained a patent and organized the Westinghouse Air Brake Company. The income from his brakes made him a millionaire by the time he was 30 years old. But that was only the beginning. Rather than sitting back and enjoying the fruits of success, Westinghouse plunged even further into his problem-solving efforts. He frequently worked 17-hour days, 6 days a week, jumping from one project to the next.

Gradually, he focused most of his energies in one area—electricity. He had learned about this new challenge while he was making improvements in railroad signal devices. Intrigued by the nature of electricity, in 1885 he bought the patents for a

Train wrecks and derailments, like this one in the 1860s (top), were not uncommon in the 19th century. Seeing a terrible train crash motivated Westinghouse to invent his air brake. The new brake was quickly put to the test when a train had to stop suddenly for a man and horse and cart (bottom). The brake worked, and Westinghouse went on to form the Westinghouse Air Brake Company.

"secondary generator" from a French investor and an English inventor. Working with William Stanley, who had done pioneer work in the field of alternating current, Westinghouse completely altered the Englishman's design and developed the transformer, the key to the alternating current system. In 1886 he formed the Westinghouse Electric Company to build equipment for the system.

At that time, other inventors were making plans to introduce electricity into the home. Their system used a form of electricity called *direct current* (DC). Although it was a safe form of electricity, direct current could not travel more than a mile from its source. *Alternating current* (AC), on the other hand, could be transmitted at very high forces, or "voltages," and could travel long distances. High-voltage electricity, however, was far more dangerous than the low-voltage direct current, and no one had been able to control it.

Thomas Edison and other scientists warned that Westinghouse was playing with people's lives by offering alternating current for homes. Edison argued that direct current electricity would greatly eliminate the risk of fire and electrocution. Although Westinghouse made alternating current electricity safe, his competitors waged a relentless campaign to scare away his customers. One ingenious trick they used was to persuade the New York legislature to carry out sentences of the death penalty with an electric chair that used Westinghouse's system. This reinforced

Competition is one of the basic features of the U.S. business system. **Competition** means trying to get something that others are also trying to get. Competition in business can occur in many ways. Producers compete for the best raw materials. Businesses compete with each other for the most customers. One way to do this is by selling a product at a lower price than other manufacturers. Another way is to provide some other kind of advantage. A candy store might give away free samples to customers, for example.

The Columbian Exposition proved the worth of AC electricity.

the image of alternating current, commonly known then as "Westinghouse current," as a deadly force.

Westinghouse realized that he needed a public display as dramatic as the life-saving trial run of his air brake to demonstrate the safety of his alternating current system. In 1893 he won a contract to provide the lighting for the massive Columbian Exposition in Chicago. More than one-quarter million lamps using alternating current glowed for six months without a single accident.

After that, Edison, General Electric, and others followed Westinghouse's lead. By the early 1900s, alternating current electricity was in widespread use in homes and businesses. Thanks to Westinghouse, no one, including the president, would ever have to be afraid again of turning on the lights.

A Motor Fueled by Love

Evinrude

A SPUTTERING ENGINE DOESN'T USUally set a romantic mood, but the development of the Evinrude outboard motor is entangled in a love story. If not for a passionate impulse, the Evinrude motor might not have been invented.

Ole Evinrude was born in Norway in 1877. When he was a child, he and his parents immigrated to a small farm in Wisconsin. Ole attended school only until the third grade, but he showed exceptional skill with his hands. At the age of 14, he secretly built his own sailboat. His father, however, considered such pursuits a waste of time. When he discovered his son's boat, which was hidden on the family property, he chopped it into firewood.

Ole built another sailboat immediately, showing the independent spirit that would soon whisk him off the farm. At the age of 16, Ole set off on his own to find work as a machinist. After working at jobs in Wisconsin, Pennsylvania, and Illinois, the youth settled in Milwaukee, Wisconsin. Like many young men who lived around the turn of the century, Ole was swept up in the excitement over the "horseless carriage," the automobile. Many inventors and mechanics at that time were working to improve the power and reliability of the existing automobile engines while reducing noise and fumes. Evinrude tried his hand at it, working in the basement of a Milwaukee boardinghouse.

His small engine turned out to be of such exceptional quality that he decided to manufacture it. With the financial backing of a friend, he formed his own company, Clemick and Evinrude.

Unfortunately, the automobile industry destroyed newcomers as fast as it attracted them. High costs, tremendous competition, and the difficulty of attracting customers in a crowded industry all made the business tough. Like most automotive enterprises begun around 1900, Evinrude's business failed.

Evinrude learned from his failure, however, and launched another business, the Motor Car Power Equipment Company. By working long hours to build a lightweight auto engine so versatile it could be installed on almost any buggy, Evinrude made his second venture more successful. The company sold so many engines that it soon needed a bookkeeper.

Ole Evinrude

The automobile **industry** refers to the group of automobile manufacturers as a whole. The word *industry* can also be used more generally to mean all of a nation's manufacturing activity.

One of the applicants for the job was a capable young woman named Bess Cary. Evinrude found her attractive as well. He was so shy, however, that he could not bring himself to hire her. Fortunately, Cary figured out what the problem was, and she volunteered to work for him.

Once Bess had broken the ice, the two began dating. They both worked long hours six days a week and saved Sunday for relaxation. During the summer, relaxation often meant a picnic. One hot Sunday in 1904, they were lolling about with friends on an island in Okauchee Lake when Bess mentioned that she wished they had brought some ice cream.

Eager to please his girlfriend, Ole insisted on granting her wish. He gallantly offered to row to shore and buy the ice cream. A strong, well-built man, he was sure he could easily row the four-mile round-trip and be back quickly. The look on Bess's face would be well worth the trouble.

But love had blinded him. The two miles into shore presented no problem, but a rare east wind had come up that afternoon. On his way back, Ole had to battle with all his might to make any headway against the wind and the waves. By the time he reached his friends, he was sweaty and exhausted and the ice cream had completely melted. The look on Bess's face was not the one he had been hoping for.

The blunder did not affect their romance (Ole and

Bess Cary

Bess were married in 1907), but Ole was so embarrassed that from then on he despised rowing. He kept wishing he could have crossed the water more quickly, even against the wind. Out of his frustration came the idea of building a motor for a boat.

Evinrude was not the first to attempt to propel a boat by mechanical means. Inventors had been experimenting with boat motors since 1873. But all previous efforts had run into problems. Though heavy and awkward, most of the motors were too weak to push any but the smallest and lightest of craft. The more powerful motors were smoky and smelly and too expensive to be practical.

With the company slipping back into financial trouble, Ole and Bess had to work harder than ever to survive. Working in what little spare time he could squeeze into his days, Ole Evinrude dabbled with the idea of a boat motor.

Finally he obtained the results he had been striving for. In April of 1907, accompanied by two brothers-in-law, he rented a rowboat and shoved off from the bank of the Kinnickinnic River in Milwaukee. Attached to the boat was a 72-pound, one-cylinder engine that Bess said looked like a coffee grinder. Evinrude had positioned his motor directly above a single, straight drive shaft that spun propellers submerged in the water. As they cruised up and down the river at a speed of about five miles per hour, Evinrude and his passengers enjoyed watching the expressions of amused onlookers.

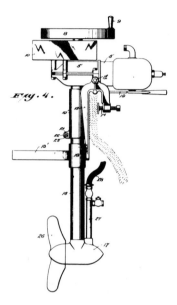

Illustration from the patent for Evinrude's motor

The motor worked fine, and Bess urged him to improve its appearance. Ole developed a more attractive design and lent the motor to a friend. The friend was so pleased with his day of effortless boating that he pulled out a wad of cash and bought 10 new motors!

Evinrude then patented his invention and formed the Evinrude Motor Company to manufacture his new product. Bess not only handled the books but also directed sales and advertising. In her first

Evinrude's new engine launched the pleasure boat industry and changed boating forever. The motor "did for water transportation what Ford's 'Tin Lizzie' did for land transportation during the first quarter of this century," said Professor J.J. Ermenc, a member of the American Society of Mechanical Engineers, in 1981. The Tin Lizzie, or automobile, created enormous changes in society.

A traveling salesman shows the popular Elto motor to a group of potential customers in Wisconsin.

advertisement, Bess wrote, "Don't row! Throw the oars away! Use an Evinrude Motor!" For most of the next few years, Ole struggled to keep up with the flood of orders.

By 1914 the Evinrude Motor Company was known throughout the world. Success did not spell the end of Ole and Bess's love story, however. When Ole saw that the frantic pace of business was wrecking Bess's health, he knew she would have to give up work. Yet he could not bear to run things by himself. After all, they had built the company from scratch and had worked together for many years. Ole decided that, if Bess had to leave her job, he would leave, too. They sold the company and retired while they

The Outboard Marine Corporation was formed as a result of a merger of different companies. A **merger** is a union of two (or more) companies in which one company buys another. In recent years, mergers (sometimes called takeovers) have become common.

were still in their thirties. For five years they relaxed, exploring the nation's waterways on a 42-foot boat that Ole designed.

Evinrude was not quite finished with the working world, however. He began tinkering with his old motor and before long had devised an improved version. The new motor was nearly twice as powerful as the original, yet the improved one weighed almost 25 pounds less and was quieter. Bess named it the Elto, which stands for Evinrude Light Twin Outboard. The rejuvenated Evinrudes organized a new company in 1920 to market this machine.

Over the next few years, Evinrude continued to make improvements in boat motors. Once again, Bess's health forced her to retire. In 1934 the man who had turned an embarrassing incident into a breakthrough in product technology died at the age of 57. In 1936 the company merged with other boat motor producers to form the Outboard Marine and Manufacturing Corporation (today the Outboard Marine Corporation).

Before the advent of precooked baby food, parents had to strain vegetables by hand, a lengthy and often frustrating process.

Birth
of a Baby Food

Gerber

ONE SUNDAY EVENING IN THE SUM-
mer of 1927, Dan and Dorothy Gerber were getting
ready to go out for the evening. They found it was
taking them longer than they had hoped. Dorothy
had to feed their seven-month-old daughter, Sally,
before they left. Dan impatiently eyed the clock as
Dorothy began to strain the peas.

Dorothy was tired of mashing vegetables through
a strainer three times a day, seven days a week. She
suggested that Dan try hand-straining the baby food
himself. The container of peas, the strainer, and the
bowl ended up in Dan's lap, and he discovered for
himself what a slow, messy, frustrating process straining vegetables was. Within 24 hours, Dan was looking
for a better way to make baby food.

Fortunately, the materials for a solution were near

Tired of making baby food at home, Dorothy Gerber urged her husband Dan to try to find a better way to make it.

at hand. Dan and his father, Frank Gerber, owned a vegetable canning factory in their small town of Fremont, Michigan. Dorothy knew that the plant already had a machine that could puree tomatoes. She wondered if any of the equipment there could also strain baby food.

When Dan went to work the next morning, he spent much of the day adapting some of the plant machinery to the task of straining peas. The more the Gerbers thought about it, the more certain they were that other parents hated the tedious straining process as much as they did. Why not design machinery to do the job in the factory and eliminate the task from the family kitchen?

The plan, however, had to be approved by the majority owner of the factory, Dan's father. Frank

Dan Gerber

By researching the market, Gerber was trying to find out how many people would buy baby food, what kind of people would buy it, and what other baby food products were already being sold. **Marketing research** is done to find out what people want and the best way to satisfy their needs. **Surveys** are a common form of marketing research. Surveys are groups of questions that researchers ask a lot of people in order to gather their views and opinions.

Gerber knew the risks involved in making products for babies. If the company ever made a mistake that caused trouble for a baby's delicate digestive system, the Fremont Canning Company could be ruined. Since the plant was doing well, it would have been easy for Frank to stick with what he was doing.

But the elder Gerber had never been one to stand still. He had risked using new processes before. With both his son and daughter-in-law arguing in favor of making strained foods, Frank Gerber gave Dan his approval.

Cautious with the family money, Dan took his time in laying the groundwork for his project. First he researched the market. Strained baby food was not a novel idea. Some brands were already on the market, but they were not selling well. These specialty products sold only in drugstores, and they cost so much that few people could afford them. National surveys showed that many people across the country were exasperated with straining baby food. If the Gerbers could maintain a high-quality product and keep it reasonably priced by selling large quantities in grocery stores, they were certain to be successful.

The next step was coming up with a good product. Frank and Dan spent nearly a year trying out various recipes and straining techniques. Babies of Fremont Canning Company employees, including Sally Gerber, sampled the concoctions and their responses were recorded.

In the fall of 1928, the Gerbers introduced their first five baby foods: peas, spinach, prunes, carrots, and vegetable soup. Dan then devised a clever plan to get the product into grocery stores. He placed an advertisement in *Good Housekeeping* magazine, offering to sell six cans of baby food for $1.00 to people who would send him the name of their local grocer. Armed with the directory of names this gave him, Dan approached the grocers and asked them to stock his products based on his evidence of the demand for baby food.

Recognizing the importance of a strong visual identity for their product, the Gerbers set up a contest for artists to submit pictures of a healthy, happy baby. One of the contestants, Dorothy Hope Smith, sent in a charcoal sketch with an attached note saying she would be happy to finish the picture if it was what the Gerbers wanted. Dan and Frank liked the sketch just as it was, and Smith's rough drawing became the famous Gerber baby.

Gerber baby food set off a storm of demand far greater than Dan had ever imagined possible. Within six months of beginning production, Gerber strained products could be found on grocery shelves across the country. The baby food did not stay long on the shelves, either. The Fremont Canning Company sold more than a half million cans of baby food during the first year of business.

Success breeds imitators, and the baby food market was no exception. Just four years after Dan Gerber

The familiar image of the smiling Gerber baby is a **trademark**—a word, name, symbol, or device used by a manufacturer to identify its products and distinguish them from other products. Only the Gerber Products Company can legally use the picture of the Gerber baby.

Getting baby food to grocery shelves across the country is what businesspeople call **distribution**—making sure a product is at the right place at the right time. A product may go directly from the manufacturer to the consumer, or it may go from the manufacturer to a store and then to a consumer (the person who buys the product).

In 1930 Gerber hired dietician Lillian Storms to develop and test recipes for the company.

broke new ground in this market, he faced more than 60 competitors. The company kept ahead of the competition by establishing a reputation as baby experts. Dorothy Gerber answered letters from consumers who wrote in with a variety of child-rearing concerns. Before long the company hired a nationally known dietician and other experts who wrote pamphlets and booklets on the care and feeding of babies.

In 1941 the name of the company was changed
from the Fremont Canning Company to the Gerber
Products Company. Since that time, most United
States parents have been happy to let food companies
handle the inconvenience of mashing food for babies.
Many families have given the task to Gerber, which
now makes more than 187 varieties of baby foods.

Few people have been as successful as the Gerbers
in "killing two birds with one stone." Not only did
they get rid of one of their most dreaded chores,
but they were able to make a fortune in the process.

Darkroom in a Box

Polaroid

EDWIN LAND KNEW MORE ABOUT cameras than most people. He had patented a light polarizer and sold it to the Eastman Kodak Company for use as a light filter in cameras.

But when Land vacationed with his family in Santa Fe, New Mexico, in 1943, he was just another tourist hoping to capture a few memories on film. When he aimed his camera at his three-year-old daughter, he was thinking more about her smile than about the mechanics of cameras. The girl posed for the picture and then posed the questions that would shape the rest of Land's life.

She wanted to see how the picture turned out. Where was it? Why would she have to wait so long before she could see it?

Land listened attentively to her complaint. He

was fond of defining creativity as the "sudden cessation of stupidity." In this case, he saw a problem so simple that it had taken a three-year-old child to see it clearly. People might be more apt to enjoy picture-taking and buy equipment if they could see the finished product right away. Land took up his daughter's challenge and began the experiments that eventually led to the growth of a large corporation.

Edwin Land was born in 1909 and carved out a unique niche in life at an early age. While still in high school, he set up a home laboratory to study the relatively untapped field of polarized light. He used filters to block certain light waves so that the intensity of the light could be controlled.

By placing polarizing filters on headlights, Edwin Land reduced glare. Polarized light has part of the light blocked out.

When he was a freshman at Harvard University, Land's experiments with polarized light took a dramatic turn. In 1926 the 17-year-old Land was walking along a busy street in New York City at night. Squinting from the glare of the headlights, he suddenly realized that the glare could be eliminated by polarizing filters. Such filters could save lives lost in accidents caused by blinding headlights.

Land immediately dropped out of school to devote his time to the project. He spent entire days at the New York Public Library, hunting up articles on polarization. At night he carried out his own experiments in the room he was renting. When he needed better equipment than he could afford, he occasionally sneaked into a laboratory at Columbia University late at night.

By 1928 the teenager had produced the world's first light polarizer in sheet form. After applying for a patent, he returned to Harvard, where he was offered the cooperation of the physics department and a large laboratory for his experiments.

To **license** an invention is to authorize another person's (or company's) use of the invention for a fee.

Impatient to carry on with his research, Land again left college before graduating. A Harvard physics professor left with him and they formed the Land-Wheelwright Laboratories in 1932. Working out of a Boston cellar, Land developed what was to become one of the most practical polarizing products—sunglasses.

After several years of licensing his inventions to

other companies, Land formed the Polaroid Corporation in 1937. The company focused on Land's long-sought goal of reducing headlight glare. The small company attracted the attention of a number of investors, who supplied Land with enough money to expand his business.

Before Land had a chance to sell his idea to Detroit automakers, World War II broke out. Both automakers and Land became preoccupied with manufacturing items for the war. Polaroid made items such as lenses and gunsights. With the end of the war, in 1945, the market for these items vanished. For various reasons, the company couldn't sell the headlight filter system. Polaroid did manufacture 3-D glasses for use in watching 3-D movies, but the company was losing money. Land decided to produce something he could "sell as directly to the consumer as possible."

Fortunately, Land had found another goal, thanks to his daughter. Following her impatient reaction to photography in 1943, Land began thinking about the problem of instant film development. In 1944 he began working on it in his spare time. By 1946 he was concentrating all his energy on meeting the seemingly impossible challenge. He would have to squeeze the whole darkroom developing process into a small, inexpensive camera.

Land came up with more than 100 original, patented ideas before the process worked. By the winter of 1947, Polaroid announced its one-step

The investors who supplied money to Land were buying shares, or portions, of stock in Land's company. A **stock** is a small part of ownership in a company. Ownership is divided among many shareholders or owners. Stocks are traded—bought and sold—in stock exchanges. The most well known stock exchange is on Wall Street in New York City.

A 1938 sales display features Polaroid "Day Glasses," or sunglasses.

The
Counter
Card 9×13"

.. They give you the view without the glare ..

The AUTOMATIC DEMONSTRATOR

SEE HOW
POLAROID*
DAY GLASSES
STOP *Reflected* GLARE

What the Customer Sees

THROUGH ORDINARY SUN GLASSES

THROUGH POLAROID DAY GLASSES

TRY
Ordinary SUNGLASSES
TRY
POLAROID Day Glasses
LET YOUR EYES DECIDE
...

developing process to a group of incredulous optical scientists. The new camera compressed the entire developing-printing process into a five-pound package.

Since Polaroid was not in the camera business itself, it offered to sell the process to existing camera and film companies. No one took the Polaroid process seriously, however. The initial sepia-toned prints (which were brown) looked old-fashioned. Almost everyone in the photography business thought of Polaroid's invention as a remarkable gimmick that would never amount to more than a novelty item.

Polaroid then decided to market its own product, the Polaroid Model 95. Its instant popularity proved that Land's daughter had not been alone; the new product attracted thousands of customers who had rarely used a camera before. Within two years of its introduction of sepia tone film, Polaroid introduced its first black and white instant film. By 1960 pictures were available in just 15 seconds. Three years later, the company developed an instant process that would work for the far more complex process of color photography.

Some fathers will do just about anything for their daughters. Because Edwin Land took his young daughter's questions seriously, he developed the product that made Polaroid one of the best-known companies in the United States.

Edwin Land demonstrates his new one-step photography at a meeting of the Optical Society of America. Although the optical scientists were skeptical at first, the new camera proved enormously successful.

Status Symbol Built Out of Love

Jacuzzi

Like most fashions, status symbols change with the times. In the 1970s, items which had long been considered luxuries, such as swimming pools, were commonplace in many neighborhoods. The time was ripe for a new luxury item. The "hot tub," a soothing bath of hot, swirling water, filled the void.

These hot tubs, which caught on so quickly in the 1970s, were commonly called "Jacuzzis." Jacuzzi is not, however, a generic name for a spa or hot tub, but the name of the company that created the first whirlpool bath for home use. Ironically, this luxury item was not developed as a toy for the wealthy but as a tool for the needy. The original Jacuzzi whirlpool pump was inspired by a father's love for his disabled son.

61

Candido Jacuzzi, born in Italy in 1903, was one of 13 children. When he was young, his six older brothers immigrated to the United States to begin their business careers. The aircraft industry, just in its infancy, looked promising to the Jacuzzis. The young men formed their own company in California in 1915 to make airplane propellers.

Their timing was fortunate. The United States' entry into World War I a few years later created an instant demand for new airplanes. With the profits they earned from a government contract to provide propellers for the military, the Jacuzzi brothers brought the rest of the family, including Candido, to the United States.

Realizing that they could not count on wooden propellers for continued earnings, the Jacuzzis delved more deeply into aircraft technology. Jacuzzi might have become as well-known a name in aircraft as Boeing or Lockheed had it not been for a tragic accident. In 1921 Giocondo Jacuzzi was killed when one of their newly designed planes crashed. The other brothers were so distraught that their interest in airplanes dissolved, and they gradually abandoned the business altogether.

It was not until 1926 that they found a new direction for their energies. That year the oldest of the Jacuzzi boys, Rachele, invented a water-injection pump. The Jacuzzis soon developed and manufactured a whole line of pumps and then branched out into filters and other water system components

The Jacuzzi brothers knew that wooden propellers were becoming obsolete. An **obsolete** product or process is no longer used because a new and better product or process has replaced it.

to meet the growing needs of agriculture and business in California.

Their business, based in Berkeley, California, flourished without much change until 1943. Before then, little had been heard from the youngest of the Jacuzzi boys, Candido. Candido and his wife had a baby boy named Kenny, who contracted a severe case of rheumatoid arthritis. This disease was painful as well as crippling, and the parents were desperate for a way to provide relief for their son's throbbing joints. The only possibility seemed to be hydrotherapy, or water therapy. To get hydrotherapy for Kenny, the Jacuzzis had to drive to a hospital that specialized in whirlpool treatments for injured World War II veterans. The soothing effects of warm,

After 1920 the Jacuzzis stopped building wooden propellers.

The Jacuzzi brothers pose in front of their new product, water pumps. From left to right: Candido, Rachele, Joseph, Frank, Valeriano. Later the pump was adapted for use as a whirlpool pump.

circulating water had been appreciated for many centuries, at least as far back as the ancient Egyptians and Greeks.

As a manufacturer of water pumps, Candido was naturally curious about how the whirlpool worked. Upon close inspection, he found that the jets that shot the water around the tub, though much smaller, were similar to jets that his company made. He thought about how much better it would be if Kenny did not have to wait for scheduled appointments and then be driven so far for every treatment. Would it be practical to build a small whirlpool bath for use in the home, so that Kenny could use it anytime he wanted?

Jacuzzi put the company engineers to work on the problem, and they soon came up with some designs. They devised a portable pump that could be moved in and out of a regular bathtub.

Other sufferers heard about the portable whirlpool pump, and the Jacuzzi Company turned out special orders for individuals. By far the largest number of whirlpools were sold to hospitals and therapy centers, though, and large, established companies held tight control over those sales.

In 1955 Jacuzzi decided to market the portable whirlpool pump as a health aid for those with severe muscle aches and diseases of the joints. With that in mind, the company sold its product through drugstores as well as bath supply shops and home demonstrations. Many of Jacuzzi's customers were athletes who enjoyed the whirlpool's healing effect on muscle pulls, aching joints, and damaged ligaments.

Eventually the company decided to enlist the aid of some glamorous entertainers to make the whirlpools appear more attractive. In the late 1950s, movie stars such as Randolph Scott and Jayne Mansfield praised the whirlpool's virtues, and

Using celebrities to sell a product is a form of advertising. **Advertising** is the presentation of ideas, goods and services to the public. This presentation is paid for by a sponsor such as Jacuzzi. **Promotion** is all of a company's selling activities, including advertising, face-to-face selling, and special efforts such as coupons or contests.

portable whirlpools were offered as prizes on the TV show "Queen for a Day."

Although sales increased enough to justify continuing production of the whirlpool, it was still only a sideline at Jacuzzi. Most of the company's income still came from water pumps and swimming pool equipment. The main drawback of the whirlpool pump was that it took up so much space in the bathtub that the user could not lie back comfortably. Unless they needed the whirlpool for health reasons, most people did not want to share their bathtub with a pump.

That problem was solved by the next generation of Jacuzzis. In 1968 Roy Jacuzzi, the grandson of

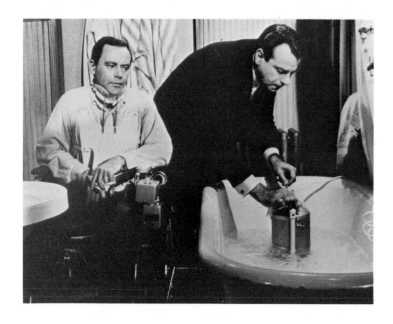

Jack Lemmon and Walter Matthau used a Jacuzzi whirlpool pump in the 1968 movie "The Odd Couple."

Roy Jacuzzi

A **status symbol** is an item which has become a sign of wealth. The person who buys this item hopes to show others that he or she can afford to spend a lot of money. Some common status symbols, besides whirlpool spas, are BMW and Mercedes cars, certain kinds of watches, and mink coats.

one of the original Jacuzzi brothers, perfected a self-contained whirlpool bath in which all the pumps and jets were hidden beneath an attractive exterior. The new product had all the ingredients of a status symbol—it was pleasurable, healthy, and showy.

Customers soon began asking for larger and larger whirlpool baths—too large to be partially filled from a water heater. By putting a heater and filter into the system, Roy Jacuzzi made a whirlpool spa for the home. The large spas could be moved away from the plumbing of the house and used outdoors. Instead of inviting friends over for a dip in the swimming pool, well-to-do people invited neighbors over to relax in the spa. So many customers purchased self-contained whirlpools from Jacuzzi that many people began to refer to any hot tub or whirlpool as a Jacuzzi.

By the time the family sold the company in 1979, the name Jacuzzi was known throughout the world. A product designed to make life bearable for a small child had been transformed to make life luxurious for thousands of adults.

Monsanto's
Magic Carpet

AstroTurf

In THE SPRING OF 1965, JUDGE ROY Hofheinz, owner of the Houston Astros baseball team, threw open the doors of the spacious palace that he proclaimed the "eighth wonder of the world." The Houston Astros baseball players gawked at their new home, the first completely domed and air-conditioned sports stadium ever built.

Fans poured in to see this bizarre, futuristic building that had done the unimaginable: made baseball into an indoor sport. More than 2,000,000 fans turned out to see the architectural novelty that season.

It was not long, however, before the wonder in the eyes of ball players faded. Outfielders looking up at the ceiling of the transparent dome felt as though they were viewing the sun reflected in a mirror. The blinding glare and the distracting steel latticework of the roof made it almost impossible to follow the flight of a fly ball. Skilled players waiting for a pop fly would suddenly cover their heads and race for safety.

For a while the players coped as best they could with the hazards of Houston's outfield. Many players wore batting helmets in the field for protection. To avoid looking straight up, the Astros' center fielder chased fly balls in left field and the left fielder went after balls hit to center field.

Finally, the transparent dome roof was painted. This solved the problem of the glare, but it caused another irritating situation. With the sunlight blocked out, the dome's grass could not grow. Even a variety of grass that had been especially chosen for its ability to grow in the shade withered in the darkened indoor arena. Again, the Astros tried to improve the situation. They laid new sod, which died as quickly as the original grass had. They even sprayed green paint on the yellowed grass. Before long the splendor of the shiny new Astrodome was marred by a field that looked like a vacant city lot.

The Astros' problem could only be solved with a drastic, innovative solution. They needed some kind of artificial turf, and they turned to the Monsanto Company for help. The huge St. Louis-based company had been founded in 1901 by John Queeny. Queeny named the company after his wife, whose maiden name was Olga Monsanto. The company had originally been formed to manufacture saccharin, an

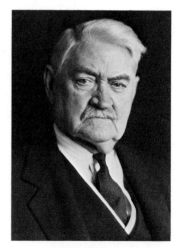

John Queeny

The Monsanto Company was not always the huge corporation it is today. Its modest beginning dates back to 1901.

A large company like Monsanto is often divided into several different units called **divisions**. Most businesses start small. The owner makes most decisions and performs most tasks. As the company grows, different activities are assigned to different people. Gradually, different activities are performed in separate areas called departments. If the department continues to grow, it may become a separate division.

artificial sweetener. After many trials and hardships, including attempts by large European chemical companies to force Monsanto out of business, the company had prospered and expanded into production of a variety of chemical products.

Monsanto's development of artificial playing surfaces happened at an opportune time. Searching for new markets for their chemical products, the company had looked into the possibility of making carpet out of synthetic, or artificial, fibers. One of Monsanto's divisions, Chemstrand, had done research in this area during the 1950s. Eventually, researchers came up with several products—including acrylic fibers and nylon—that were more durable than, but just as attractive as, regular carpets. Some of these synthetic carpets were so durable that Monsanto explored the possibility of using them outdoors for golf greens and patios. No one, however, thought seriously of carpeting entire stadiums.

At the same time, the Ford Foundation, a non-profit organization, was providing funds to large corporations for research into artificial turf. The Foundation had conducted a study which found

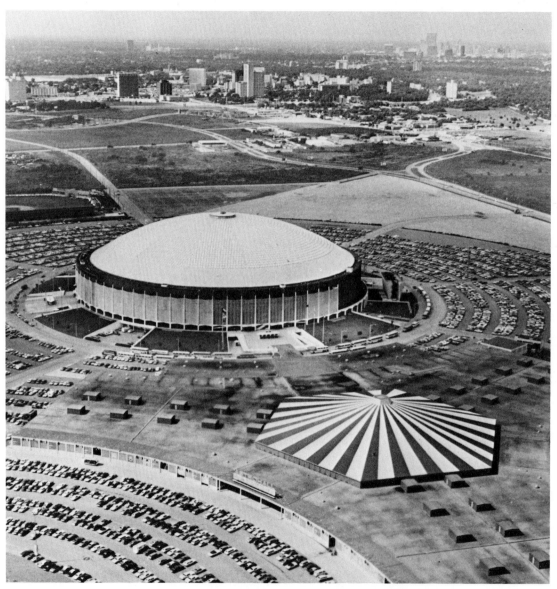

The Houston Astrodome was the first domed stadium built in the U.S.

Like Monsanto did, many companies spend large amounts of money on research and development. **Research** is investigation aimed at discovering new scientific knowledge. **Development** is the attempt to use new knowledge to make useful products or processes. Computer and automobile companies spend some of the highest amounts of money on research and development.

that children in small towns and rural areas were in better shape than their city counterparts, because of the lack of good playing fields in urban areas.

With its previous experience in synthetic fibers and carpets, Monsanto made rapid strides in this research. In 1964 Monsanto developed a new kind of carpet with a texture similar to a stiff hairbrush. The company called the material "Chemgrass." Chemgrass met the Ford Foundation's requirements for a surface that would look and feel like grass, yet withstand years of heavy use. The experimental surface was installed at the Moses Brown School, a private high school in Providence, Rhode Island, in 1964. Although the surface was crude by today's standards, the experiment did prove that artificial turf could work.

Judge Hofheinz of the Houston Astros found out about the experiment at Moses Brown and asked Monsanto to develop an artificial turf for the Astrodome as soon as possible. Working around the clock, Monsanto produced enough of the new turf to cover the infield by the start of the 1966 baseball season. The first test came in an exhibition game between the Astros and the Los Angeles Dodgers on March 19, 1966. Infielders praised the sure footing and true bounce of the artificial grass, and Astros officials decided to convert the outfield as well. The media dubbed the new surface "AstroTurf," and the name stuck. By July 9 of that season, the outfield carpet was in place and ready for use.

In 1967 AstroTurf was installed in outdoor stadiums in Seattle, Washington, and Terre Haute, Indiana. AstroTurf drained rainwater well, did not get muddy, provided a fast surface, could be used day after day without wearing out, and cost little to maintain. In 1967 National Football League Commissioner Pete Rozelle predicted that within 10 years all professional football fields would be artificial. Within the next 11 years, 10 more baseball stadiums were artificially

Baseball players adapted quickly to using AstroTurf. Today, it is used in many stadiums around the country.

surfaced. Monsanto seemed to have found a product that suited everyone.

The early glowing predictions have sinced cooled down, however. There has been some controversy about injuries related to artificial turf, and a few parks that had installed artificial turf have gone back to grass. Also, despite AstroTurf's fame, the product was never an important profit maker for Monsanto. In 1988 Monsanto sold the AstroTurf Division to Balsam Sportstattenbau, a West German manufacturer of sports and recreational surfaces.

Even so, when Monsanto's AstroTurf solved an embarrassing problem for the Houston Astrodome, a new era in sports began. Because of Astroturf's toughness and versatility, the professional and collegiate sports worlds have not been the same since.

For Further Reading...

Bryant, K.L., Jr. and Dethloff, H.C. *A History of American Business.* Prentice-Hall Inc., 1983.

Clary, D.C. *Great American Brands.* Fairchild Books, 1981.

Fucini, J.J. and Fucini, S. *Entrepreneurs: The Men and Women Behind Famous Brand Names.* G.K. Hall, 1985.

Livesay, H.C. *American Made: Men Who Shaped the American Economy.* Little, Brown & Company, 1980.

Moskowitz, M., Katz, M. and Levering, R., eds. *Everybody's Business.* Harper and Row, 1980.

Slappey, S.G. *Pioneers of American Business.* Grosset & Dunlap, 1970.

Sobel, R. and Sicilia, D.B. *The Entrepreneurs: An American Adventure.* Houghton Mifflin Company, 1986

Thompson, J. *The Very Rich Book.* William Morrow & Company, 1981.

Vare, E. and Ptacek, G. *Mothers of Invention: From the Bra to the Bomb: Forgotten Women and Their Unforgettable Ideas.* William Morrow & Company, 1988.

INDEX

Words in **boldface** are defined in the text.

ACKNOWLEDGEMENTS

The photographs and illustrations in this book are reproduced through the courtesy of: pp. 1, 12, 15, 16, Deere & Company; pp. 2, 53, 54, 57, 59, Polaroid Corporate Archives; p. 8, Edward J. Breck; pp. 10, 11, Beatrice/Hunt-Wesson; pp. 19, 24, The Prudential Insurance Company of America; p. 21, Museum of the City of New York, Byron Collection; pp. 26, 29, P.M.I. Food Equipment Group, Troy, Ohio; p. 32 (left), U.S. Department of the Interior, National Park Service, Edison National Historic Site; pp. 32 (right), 35 (bottom), 37, Westinghouse Historical Collection; p. 35 (top), National Archives; pp. 38, 40, 41, 43, 44, Outboard Marine Corporation; pp. 46, 48, 49, 50, 51, 52, 80, Gerber Products Company; pp. 60, 63, 64, 66, 67, Jacuzzi Inc.; pp. 69, 72, 74, The Houston Astros; pp. 70, 71, The Monsanto Company.

Cover illustration by Stephen Clement.

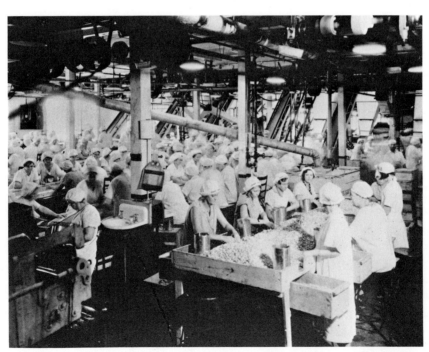

Workers at the Gerber factory in 1934 inspect produce before it is used to make baby food.